Sports Illustrated KIDS

KNOW THE STATS

FOOTBALL
IS A NUMBERS GAME

by Shane Frederick

CAPSTONE PRESS
a capstone imprint

Sports Illustrated Kids Know the Stats are published by Capstone Press,
a Capstone Imprint, 1710 Roe Crest Drive, North Mankato, Minnesota 56003.
www.mycapstone.com

Library of Congress Cataloging-in-Publication Data
is available on the Library of Congress website:
ISBN: 978-1-5435-0610-5 (library binding)
ISBN: 978-1-5435-0618-1 (eBook PDF)

Editorial Credits
Nate LeBoutillier, editor; Brent Slingsby, designer;
Eric Gohl, media researcher; Laura Manthe, production specialist

Photo Credits
Newscom: Icon SMI/Rich Gabrielson, 24, Icon Sportswire/Ken Murray, 28, Icon Sportswire/
Matthew Pearce, 16, TNS/Carlos Gonzalez, 9, UPI/Khaled Sayed, 23, USA Today Sports/Mark J.
Rebilas, 18; Sports Illustrated: Al Tielemans, 5, 26, David E. Klutho, 10, Robert Beck, 20, Simon Bruty,
cover, 7, 13, 14

Design Elements: Shutterstock

All statistics have been updated through the 2016 NFL season.

Printed in the United States of America.
010782S18

TABLE OF
CONTENTS

STATS & STORIES

Inside the Numbers

There is no doubt that LeGarrette Blount was one of the best running backs in the National Football League (NFL) in 2016. At the end of the 16-game regular season, he led the league with 18 rushing touchdowns. That was the most by any runner since 2006. Blount was a big reason why his team, the New England Patriots, returned to the Super Bowl for a record ninth time and won the championship for the fifth time.

But was Blount the best running back in the entire NFL in 2016? Let's take a closer look at some more of his stats. Blount rushed for 1,161 yards, but that was only the eighth-best total in the league. Rookie Ezekiel Elliott of the Dallas Cowboys led the NFL with 1,631 yards, 470 yards more than Blount. Elliot also scored 15 touchdowns, which was impressive but three less than Blount. Then there was David Johnson of the Arizona Cardinals. He rushed for 1,239 yards and scored 16 touchdowns on the ground. He also had four receiving TDs and led the league with 20 TDs overall. He also led the NFL in all-purpose yards. So . . . which running back would you want on your team?

LeGarrette Blount, running back,
New England Patriots

Statistics show the details in sports beyond simple wins and losses. They can explain *why* a team won or lost. They can explain *how* a player rose to a challenge — or failed to do so. They can show *which* players helped or hurt their team's chances at postseason glory. Knowing the numbers and stats will help you better understand the game — and appreciate it too!

CHAPTER ONE
OFFENSE

Points and Yards

Each time Matt Ryan approached the line of scrimmage in 2016, he had many options to make the Atlanta Falcons' offense go. The quarterback could pass the ball to receivers such as the dangerous Julio Jones or the sure-handed Mohamed Sanu. He could hand off or even throw to speedy running back Devonta Freeman too.

Led by Ryan, the 2016 season's Most Valuable Player (MVP), the Falcons were the highest-scoring team in the NFL. They scored 540 points and averaged nearly 34 points per game, the seventh-best mark in NFL history. They scored 38 touchdowns through the air and 20 more on the ground.

While points, ultimately, are the most important stat, total offense in football is measured by yards gained. The Falcons averaged 415.8 yards per game. The New Orleans Saints led the way with 426 yards per game. By the end of the season, though, the Falcons were in the Super Bowl. The Saints didn't even make the playoffs.

Matt Ryan, quarterback, Atlanta Falcons

All-Time Highest-Scoring Offenses

	Team	Year
Rank: 01	Denver Broncos	2013
Rank: 02	New England Patriots	2007
Rank: 03	Green Bay Packers	2011
Rank: 04	New England Patriots	2012
Rank: 05	Minnesota Vikings	1998

Points Per Game

01	02	03	04	05
37.87	36.81	35.00	34.81	34.75

The Passing Game

Give Drew Brees a little time in the pocket, and he can put the ball almost anywhere he wants. The New Orleans Saints quarterback is the most accurate passer in NFL history. In his first 16 seasons in the league he completed 66.6 percent of his throws. That means two of every three of his passes were caught.

Completion percentage is calculated by dividing the number of completed passes by the number of attempted passes. Take Brees' best season, 2011, for example. That season, Brees completed 468 of 657 passes. That's 71.2 percent!

Brees owns three of the top nine most accurate passing seasons in NFL history, completing 70 percent or more of his passes in each. And Brees throws a lot. He also owns five of the top eight all-time passing yardage seasons. He chucked the ball more than 5,000 yards in each of those five seasons, including 5,476 yards in 2011. That number stood as a record until Peyton Manning, playing for the Denver Broncos, edged him by one yard in 2013.

Fact

The Minnesota Vikings' Sam Bradford set the record for highest single-season completion percentage at 71.6 percent in 2016. He bested the previous top two marks, both set by Drew Brees.

Best Completion Percentage, Season

	Player	Team	Year
Rank: 01	Sam Bradford	Vikings	2016
Rank: 02	Drew Brees	Saints	2011
Rank: 03	Drew Brees	Saints	2009
Rank: 04	Ken Anderson	Bengals	1982
Rank: 05	Sammy Baugh	Redskins	1945

Completion Percentage

01	02	03	04	05
71.55%	71.23%	70.62 %	70.55 %	70.32 %

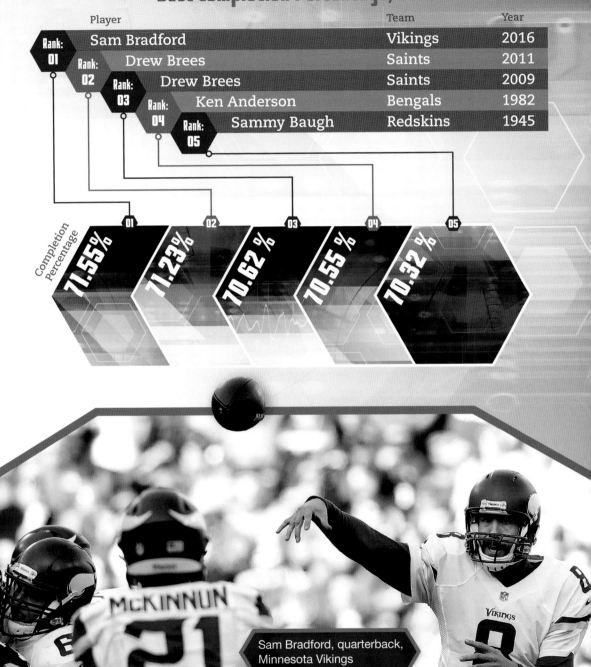

Sam Bradford, quarterback, Minnesota Vikings

Quarterbacks Rule

It's easy to see that the Green Bay Packers' Aaron Rodgers is one of the best quarterbacks in the game today. Rodgers, who has won a Super Bowl and an MVP award, throws a lot of touchdown passes and very few interceptions. With a strong arm and a quick release of the ball, Rodgers completes a high percentage of his passes and racks up plenty of yards through the air.

Aaron Rodgers, quarterback, Green Bay Packers

If that's not enough to make a strong case for him, the NFL puts all of those statistics — completions, attempts, yards, touchdowns, and interceptions — into a complex mathematical formula to determine a quarterback's passer rating. Completed passes and scoring plays help the rating; incompletions and turnovers hurt.

A passer rating greater than 100 is terrific, and, through 2016, Rodgers was the only quarterback in NFL history with a career rating that high, at 104.1. Rodgers also has the highest single-season rating of 122.5 in 2011, his MVP season.

Fact

A perfect quarterback rating is 158.3.

Best Passer Rating, Career

Rank	Player	Team	Years	Rating
01	Aaron Rodgers	Packers	2005–2016*	104.1
02	Russell Wilson	Seahawks	2012–2016*	99.6
03	Tom Brady	Patriots	2000–2016*	97.2
04	Tony Romo	Cowboys	2004–2016	97.1
05	Steve Young	Bucs, 49ers	1985–1999	96.8

* active player

Quite the Catch

Defensive coaches must go crazy planning how they're going to play the Pittsburgh Steelers in passing situations. The Steelers' opponents know who's usually going to get the ball. Stopping that player, though, is another matter. Wide receiver Antonio Brown is quarterback Ben Roethlisberger's favorite target, and Brown is a reliable one.

Only one player in NFL history has had more catches in a single season than Brown. That was the Colts' Marvin Harrison in 2002, when he hauled in 143 passes from Peyton Manning. Brown's 136 receptions in 2015 and 129 catches in 2014 rank second and fourth on the all-time list. Brown once caught 17 passes in a single game. (Brandon Marshall holds the record with 21 receptions in a single game for the Broncos in 2009.)

In more recent years, statisticians have tracked how many times receivers are targeted. A target is the intended receiver on a given play, whether he catches the ball or not. The year Brown caught **136** passes, he was targeted **193** times, meaning 57 passes thrown to Brown did not end up in his hands.

Brown's catch rate (receptions ÷ targets) was **70.5** that year. Some observers also track receivers' drop rate (dropped balls ÷ catchable passes).

Receptions

Targets

136   **193**

136 ÷ 193 = 0.705

Most Receptions, Single Season

Rank	Player	Team	Year	Average
01	Marvin Harrison	Colts	2002	143
02 Tie	Antonio Brown	Steelers	2015	136
02	Julio Jones	Falcons	2015	136
04	Antonio Brown	Steelers	2014	129
05 Tie	Herman Moore	Lions	1995	123
05	Wes Welker	Patriots	2009	123

Antonio Brown, wide receiver, Pittsburgh Steelers

Julio Jones, wide receiver, Atlanta Falcons

Reliable Receivers

Covering receiver Julio Jones can be a nightmare for opposing defensive backs. At 6-foot-3, he's tall. And he's also one of the fastest wideouts in the game. The Atlanta Falcons rely on him, throwing the ball his direction several times each game. And he racks up the catches and the yards, helping Atlanta get into scoring position.

Besides catches, receivers' work is measured in yards. In 2015 Jones moved the ball a total of 1,871 yards on receptions. That amounted to the second-best total of all time — behind the Lions' Calvin Johnson's 1,964 receiving yards in 2012. With 136 receptions in 2015, Jones averaged 13.8 yards per catch.

A receiver's yards include the distance the pass traveled through the air, so it's also important to measure what the player does after he hauls in the ball. Yards after catch (YAC) are tracked from the spot a player makes the catch until he is tackled, runs out of bounds, scores or loses the ball. In 2015 more than 37 percent of Jones' yards — 679 of 1,871 — came after he caught the ball.

Receiving Yards Per Game, Career

Rank	Player	Team	Years
01	Julio Jones	Falcons	2011–2016*
02	Odell Beckham	Giants	2014–2016*
03	Calvin Johnson	Lions	2007–2015
04	A.J. Green	Bengals	2011–2016*
05	Antonio Brown	Steelers	2010–2016*

* active player

01 — 96.3
02 — 95.9
03 — 86.1
04 — 83.0
05 — 82.9

The Rush Is On

In 2016 a pair of rookies led the Dallas Cowboys to a 13-3 record, second-best in the league. One was quarterback Dak Prescott, and the other was running back Ezekiel Elliott. The fourth overall pick in that year's draft, Elliott burst onto the scene to lead the NFL in rushing. He pounded out 1,631 yards on the ground. Divide that number by 16 games, and he averaged 108.7 yards per game.

After impressive long runs and touchdowns, Elliott pretended to spoon food into his mouth. It was his way of saying, "Feed me the ball." The Cowboys gave "Zeke" healthy portions. He carried the ball 322 times and bit off huge chunks of yards, averaging 5.1 yards per attempt.

Dak Prescot (left) and Ezekiel Elliott, Dallas Cowboys

Rushers rely on their linemen to block and open holes in the defense, but the best backs help themselves. Yards after contact are tracked, too, and Elliott was a bruiser. He broke tackles and gained nearly 1,000 of his yards after being touched by a defender.

Fact

In 2007 running back Adrian Peterson set the single-game record for rushing yards with 296. In 2012 Peterson came up 8 yards short of the Eric Dickerson's single-season record of 2,105 rushing yards.

Most Rushing Yards, Single Season

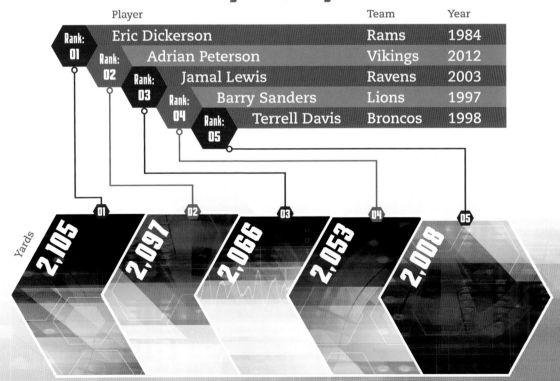

Player	Team	Year
Rank: 01 — Eric Dickerson	Rams	1984
Rank: 02 — Adrian Peterson	Vikings	2012
Rank: 03 — Jamal Lewis	Ravens	2003
Rank: 04 — Barry Sanders	Lions	1997
Rank: 05 — Terrell Davis	Broncos	1998

Yards

01 — 2,105
02 — 2,097
03 — 2,066
04 — 2,053
05 — 2,008

David Johnson, running back,
Arizona Cardinals

All-Around Performers

David Johnson's position is listed as running back, but he's more like a Swiss Army knife for the Arizona Cardinals. Johnson runs the ball, catches the ball, and, from time to time, returns kicks. Putting all of that together, his yards add up.

Johnson led the NFL in all-purpose yards in 2016 with 2,118 yards. That included 1,239 rushing yards on 293 attempts and 879 receiving yards on 80 catches. A year earlier, as a rookie, Johnson recorded 1,636 all-purpose yards — 581 rushing, 457 receiving, and 598 returning.

In 2011 speedy Saints running back Darren Sproles set the NFL record for all-purpose yards with 2,696. The triple-threat player had 603 rushing yards, 710 receiving yards, and 1,383 return yards, with 10 touchdowns.

All-Purpose Yards, Single Season

Rank	Player	Team	Year	Yards
Rank: 01	Darren Sproles	Saints	2011	2,696
Rank: 02	Derrick Mason	Titans	2000	2,690
Rank: 03	Michael Lewis	Saints	2002	2,647
Rank: 04	Lionel James	Chargers	1985	2,535
Rank: 05	Fred Jackson	Bills	2009	2,516

Fact

During a single game for the Broncos in 1995, Glyn Milburn racked up a record 404 all-purpose yards — 131 on the ground, 45 through the air, 133 returning kicks, and 95 returning punts. Surprisingly, he scored no touchdowns that day.

CHAPTER TWO

DEFENSE

Defending the Turf

The Seattle Seahawks boasted some of the best defenses of the early 2010s. Led by "Legion of Boom" defensive backs Richard Sherman, Kam Chancellor, and Earl Thomas, the Seahawks were a top-five defense from 2012 to 2016. They had the number one-ranked D in 2013 and 2014.

During those seasons, they were the only team to allow fewer than 300 yards per game. Opponents mustered only 4,274 yards in 2014, an average of 267.1 each game.

Richard Sherman, defensive back, Seattle Seahawks

As with offense, total defense is measured by yards allowed. However, when it comes to wins and losses, the most important statistic is points allowed. Seattle was even better in that category, leading the NFL from 2012 to 2015. In 2013, the year Seattle won the Super Bowl, the Seahawks allowed just 14.4 points per game.

One way to keep points off the board is by taking away the football. Interceptions and fumble recoveries can decide outcomes of games. Even the fear of a turnover can cause coaches to alter their plans. In 2014 quarterbacks threw the ball Sherman's way just 65 times, even though he was on the field for 552 passing plays. He still nabbed four interceptions and broke up 12 other passes that year.

Super D

The fewest points allowed in a single 16-game regular season is 165 points (10.3 per game), by the Baltimore Ravens in 2000. The Ravens went on to win the Super Bowl, and their defense led the way. In the Super Bowl, linebacker Ray Lewis won MVP honors. Only ten defenders have won MVP in more than 50 Super Bowls.

Fewest Average Points Allowed, Team Defense, 2016

Rank	Team	Rating
01	Patriots	15.6
02	Giants	17.8
03	Seahawks	18.3
04	Broncos	18.6
05	Cowboys	19.1

Defense Wins Championships

In the first 51 Super Bowls, a defensive player was named the game's MVP just nine times. In Super Bowl 50, Denver Broncos linebacker Von Miller earned that award for a dominating performance that led his team to a 24-10 victory over the Carolina Panthers. Miller was in on 2.5 sacks of quarterback Cam Newton and forced two fumbles. One of those fumbles led to teammate Malik Jackson's recovery for a Broncos touchdown.

Defensive players' ultimate goal is to stop the opponent from advancing the ball. They do that by tackling — knocking the ball carrier to the ground. Total tackles are the sum of solo tackles and assisted tackles. Assists are plays in which more than one player brings down the runner. Statisticians also measure tackles for loss. They come when a ballcarrier gets hit and goes down behind the line of scrimmage. The carrier might be a runner who gets stopped in his tracks or a quarterback who gets tackled before he can release a pass.

Houston Texans defensive end and sack master J.J. Watt has won three Defensive Player of the Year awards. Watt pulled down the award in 2012, 2014, and 2015, leading the league in sacks in two of those three seasons. In 2014 Watt even played a key role on the offensive side of the ball, catching three TD passes.

Single-Season Sacks (since 1982)

Rank	Player	Team	Year	Sacks
01	Michael Strahan	Giants	2001	22.5
02 Tie	Jared Allen	Vikings	2011	22.0
02 Tie	Mark Gastineau	Jets	1984	22.0
02	Justin Houston	Chiefs	2014	22.0
05 Tie	Chris Doleman	Vikings	1989	21.0
05	Reggie White	Eagles	1987	21.0

Von Miller, linebacker, Denver Broncos

CHAPTER THREE

SPECIAL TEAMS

Happy Returns

With his foot just inches away from the back of the end zone, Vikings receiver Cordarrelle Patterson caught the game-opening kickoff during a 2013 game against the archrival Packers. Instead of kneeling down for a touchback, the rookie took off. What looked like a mistake turned out to be a history-making play. Patterson sprinted straight up the middle of the field, past his blockers, and through the Packers' porous coverage. Soon he was at the other end of the field for a touchdown.

Cordarelle Patterson, returner, Minnesota Vikings

An NFL field is 100 yards long, goal line to goal line, with end zones 10 yard deep at each end. Since Patterson's play started in the back of an end zone, it officially went down as a 109-yard return, the longest scoring play in NFL history.

Offensive plays are measured from the line of scrimmage, meaning the longest one can be 99 yards. Returns, which include kickoffs, punts, and turnovers, can exceed 100 yards if they begin in the end zone.

The San Diego Chargers' Antonio Cromartie also scored on a 109-yard play, returning a missed field goal for a touchdown in 2007.

Combined Kick and Punt Return TDs, Career

Rank	Player	Teams	Years
01	Devin Hester	Bears, Falcons	2006–2016*
02	Brian Mitchell	Redskins, Eagles, Giants	1990–2003
03	Eric Metcalf	7 teams	1989–2002
03	Dante Hall	Chiefs, Rams	2000–2008
05	Josh Cribbs	Browns, Jets, Colts	2005–2014

Tie

* active player

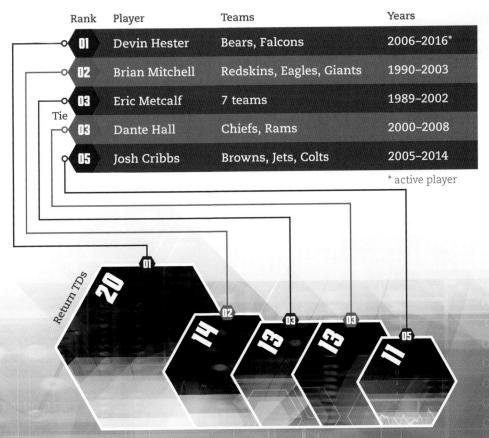

Return TDs

01 — 20
02 — 14
03 — 13
03 — 13
05 — 11

Clutch Kickers

Football fans don't always like it when the outcome of a game comes down to a field goal. If the kicker can boot the ball through the 18-foot, 6-inch-wide opening between the uprights of the goalpost, he can win the game. A miss could mean a loss. The New England Patriots had no problem putting the outcome of a Super Bowl on the foot of kicker Adam Vinatieri. Twice in his career he nailed Super Bowl-winning kicks.

Matt Prater, kicker, Denver Broncos

Kickers keep getting better and better. In his first four professional seasons, Baltimore Ravens' Justin Tucker made 89.8 percent of his field-goal tries. That put him atop the all-time list in success rate (made field goals ÷ attempted field goals).

Tucker missed just one field goal in 39 tries for a 97.4 percent success rate in 2016. He was also a perfect 27 for 27 on extra-point attempts, despite a rule change that made the point after touchdown (PAT) tougher. A season earlier the NFL had moved the PAT spot from the 2-yard line to the 15-yard line. Overall, the number of misses jumped after the change, but Tucker seemed to have no trouble.

Longest Field Goals

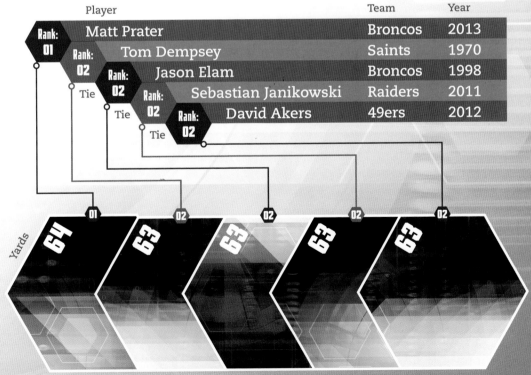

	Player	Team	Year
Rank: 01	Matt Prater	Broncos	2013
Rank: 02	Tom Dempsey	Saints	1970
Tie Rank: 02	Jason Elam	Broncos	1998
Tie Rank: 02	Sebastian Janikowski	Raiders	2011
Tie Rank: 02	David Akers	49ers	2012

Yards: 64 (01), 63 (02), 63 (02), 63 (02), 63 (02)

Time to Punt

Punting is not a glamorous job in football, but it's an important one. When a team is facing fourth down and is out of scoring range, it has to give the ball back to its opponent. A punter can help by pinning the other team deep in its own end of the field.

The best punters kick the ball high and far with the hope of limiting a long run by the return man. They also try to place the ball inside the 20-yard line without it going into the end zone for a touchback. You don't see too many punters celebrate those impressive kicks, but Oakland Raiders punter Marquette King is an exception. King often dances and poses after his punts — just like some of his teammates do when they score touchdowns.

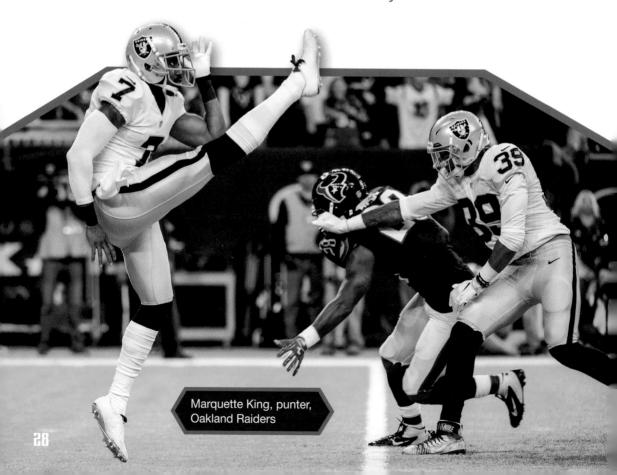

Marquette King, punter, Oakland Raiders

Punts are measured in two ways: gross yardage and net yardage. Gross yardage goes from the line of scrimmage to the point where the ball is caught or downed, goes out of bounds or into the end zone, or is declared dead. Net yardage subtracts return yards and touchbacks from the gross.

Fact

Steve O'Neal of the New York Jets had a 98-yard punt in 1969. Kicking from his team's own 1-yard line, the ball went 75 yards in the air, then bounced and rolled to the opposite 1-yard line, where it was downed.

Best Yards Per Punt Average, Career

Rank	Player	Team	Years	Rating
01	Shane Lechler	Raiders, Texans	2000–2016*	47.5
02	Thomas Morestead	Saints	2000–2016*	47.0
03	Johnny Hekker	Rams	2000–2016*	46.9
03	Sam Martin	Lions	2000–2016*	46.9
05	Marquette King	Raiders	2000–2016*	46.7

Tie

* active player

GLOSSARY

all-purpose yards—combined total yards gained by rushing, receiving, or kick or punt returns

completion percentage—statistic used to determine effectiveness of a quarterback by figuring the total percentage of pass attempts he completes to his receiver

passer rating—statistic to measure quarterbacks based on a formula that takes into account completion percentage and yards, touchdowns, and interceptions per attempt

point after touchdown (PAT)—play occurring after the scoring of a touchdown that can be worth one or two points

reception—the act of catching a football

rushing—the act of running while in possession of the football

special teams—units that take the field during kickoffs, punts, and field goal attempts

statistician—a person who collects and studies statistics

touchback—a ball that a player downs deliberately behind his own goal line or that is kicked or punted through the end zone

yards after catch (YAC)—distance gained by a receiver after catching a pass

READ MORE

The Editors of Sports Illustrated Kids. *Sports Illustrated Kids Big Book of Who: Football*. New York: Sports Illustrated, 2013.

Frederick, Shane. *Football Stats and the Stories Behind Them: What Every Fan Needs to Know*. Sports Stats and Stories. North Mankato, Minn.: Capstone Press, 2016.

Hetrick, Hans. *Six Degrees of Peyton Manning: Connecting Football Stars*. Six Degrees of Sports. North Mankato, Minn.: Capstone Press, 2015.

INTERNET SITES

Use FactHound to find internet sites related to this book.

Visit **www.facthound.com**

Just type in **9781543506099** and go.

 Check out projects, games and lots more at **www.capstonekids.com**

INDEX